"Are not women born as free as men?"

"Does it follow that 'tis right to enslave a man because he is black?"

James Otis

wrote in May, 1764, "that by the united application of all who are aggrieved, all may happily obtain redress." Soon a congress* from the colonies for the defense of their rights and privileges was organized. This Stamp Act Congress met in New York City on October 7, 1765, and a Chairman was elected. James Otis lost by one vote, yet he was the "soul" of the Congress. A Congress had met earlier, in Albany in 1754, with delegates from the northern colonies. Their Plan of Union, described by Benjamin Franklin, was that "one General Government may be formed in America...including all the said colonies...who shall meet for the first time at the City of Philadelphia, in Pennsylvania, being called by the President General...union of the colonies is absolutely necessary for their preservation." The Stamp Act was seen by the colonists as leading to "the total subversion of the British constitution and American Liberty." Due to the protests of the Stamp Act Congress, an Act of Parliament for the repeal of the Stamp Act was brought to Boston on May 16, 1766. This was, as John Adams wrote, "the triumph of Otis and his party."

*The word *congress* is from Latin and means a coming together, a meeting.

Timothy Ruggles

The Stamp Act Congress, October 7–25, 1765

The House of Representatives of the Province of Massachusetts Bay had called this Congress from the Several British Colonies and sent three delegates. Brigadier Ruggles was one and was voted Chairman. He was a powerful lawyer and loyal to the Crown. Nine colonies sent representatives to the Congress (the word Congress was used from the first day), and a petition, "Essential Rights and Liberties of the Colonists," was to be drawn up to be sent to the King and Parliament. "Otis says that when they came to sign (what was now called 'The Petition of the Freeholders and other Inhabitants of the Colonies'), Ruggles moved that none of them should sign, but that the petitions should be carried back to the Assemblies to see if they would adopt them. This would have defeated the whole enterprise. This Ruggles has an inflexible oddity about him which has gained him a character for courage and probity, but renders him a disgreeable companion in business," wrote John Adams. Ruggles challenged delegate McKean, a future president, to a duel over this. Six days after the Congress ended, New York merchants, some of whom had been delegates, signed an agreement to boycott trade with Great Britain. The Stamp Act was soon repealed.

1. Peyton Randolph

September 5, 1774 – October 22, 1774

September 5, 1774, "Monday. At Ten, the Delegates all met at the City Tavern, and walked to Carpenters Hall...then Mr. Lynch arose and said...the Honorable Peyton Randolph, Esqr., one of the Delegates from Virginia, and late Speaker of their House of Burgesses, should be appointed Chairman and he doubted not that it would be unanimous. The Question was put and he was unanimously chosen. Mr. Randolph then took the Chair." —*John Adams,* Diary. "A Question was then put what Title the Convention should assume & it was agreed that it should be called *the Congress*. Another Question was put what should be the style of Mr. Randolph & it was agreed he should be called the *President*." —*James Duane,* September 5, 1774

"The Glorious Congress of 1774"—*J. Q. Adams*

Carpenters' Hall, Philadelphia

"Then Mr. Lynch proposed that Mr. Charles Thomson a gentleman of Family, Fortune, and Character in this city should be appointed Secretary, which was accordingly done without opposition...This Charles Thomson is the Sam Adams of Philadelphia–the Life of the Cause of Liberty, they say...By a computation made this evening by Mr. McKean, there will be at this Congress about fifty-six members, twenty-two of them lawyers." —*John Adams,* Diary.

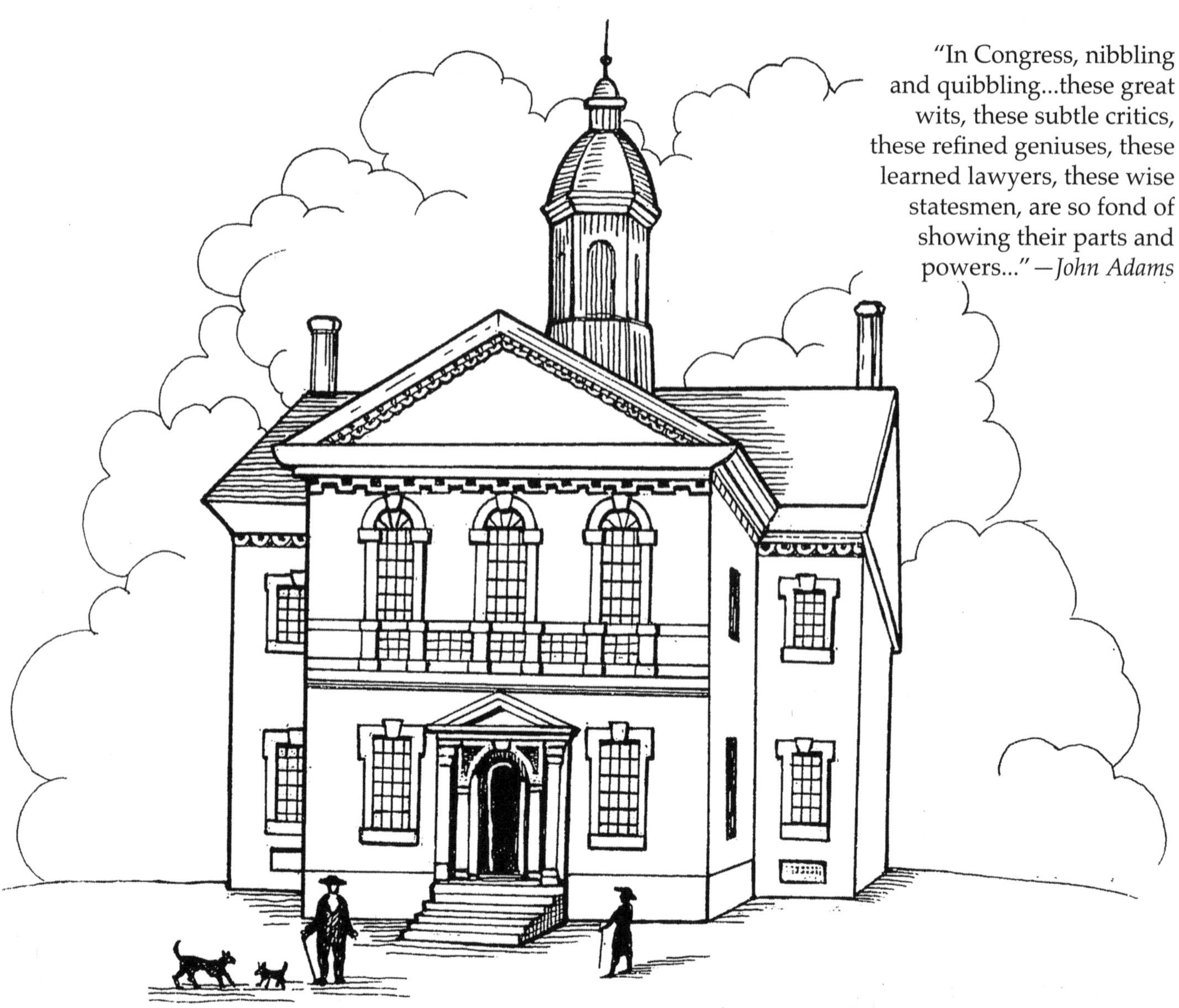

"In Congress, nibbling and quibbling...these great wits, these subtle critics, these refined geniuses, these learned lawyers, these wise statesmen, are so fond of showing their parts and powers..." —*John Adams*

"Our President (Randolph) seems designed by Nature, for the Business; of an affable, open & majestic deportment, large in size, though not out of Proportion, he commands respect & Esteem, by his aspect, independent of the high Character he sustains."—*Silas Deane*, September 5. "The Question is whether the Rights and Liberties of America shall be contended for, or given up to arbitrary Power...I hope future Ages will quote our Proceedings with Applause."—*John Adams,* September 6, 1774.

2. Henry Middleton, President for Five Days

At the end of the First Congress, October 22–26, 1774

"The Honorable P. Randolph Esqr. Being unable to attend the congress on account of indisposition, the Honorable H. Middleton Esqr. was chosen to supply his place as President...Resolved, as the opinion of this congress that it will be necessary that a congress should be held on the 10th of May next...at the city of Philadelphia and that all the Colonies in North America chuse deputies as soon as possible to attend such congress."—*Secretary Charles Thomson*, October 22, 1774.

"I dreaded the danger of disunion...people began to see that independence was approaching...the balance lay with South Carolina," wrote John Adams; that was why Middleton had been chosen.

from South Carolina

"September 8, in the Committee for stating rights, grievances, and means of redress, Colonel Lee said, 'The rights are built on a fourfold foundation: on nature, on the British constitution, on charters, and on immemorial usage'... I have ever thought we might reduce our rights to one: exemption from all laws made by the British Parliament since the emigration of our ancestors...I am well aware that my arguments tend to an independency of the Colonies...The more we conversed...the more we were encouraged to hope for a general union of the continent."—*John Adams,* Diary

The Pennsylvania State House

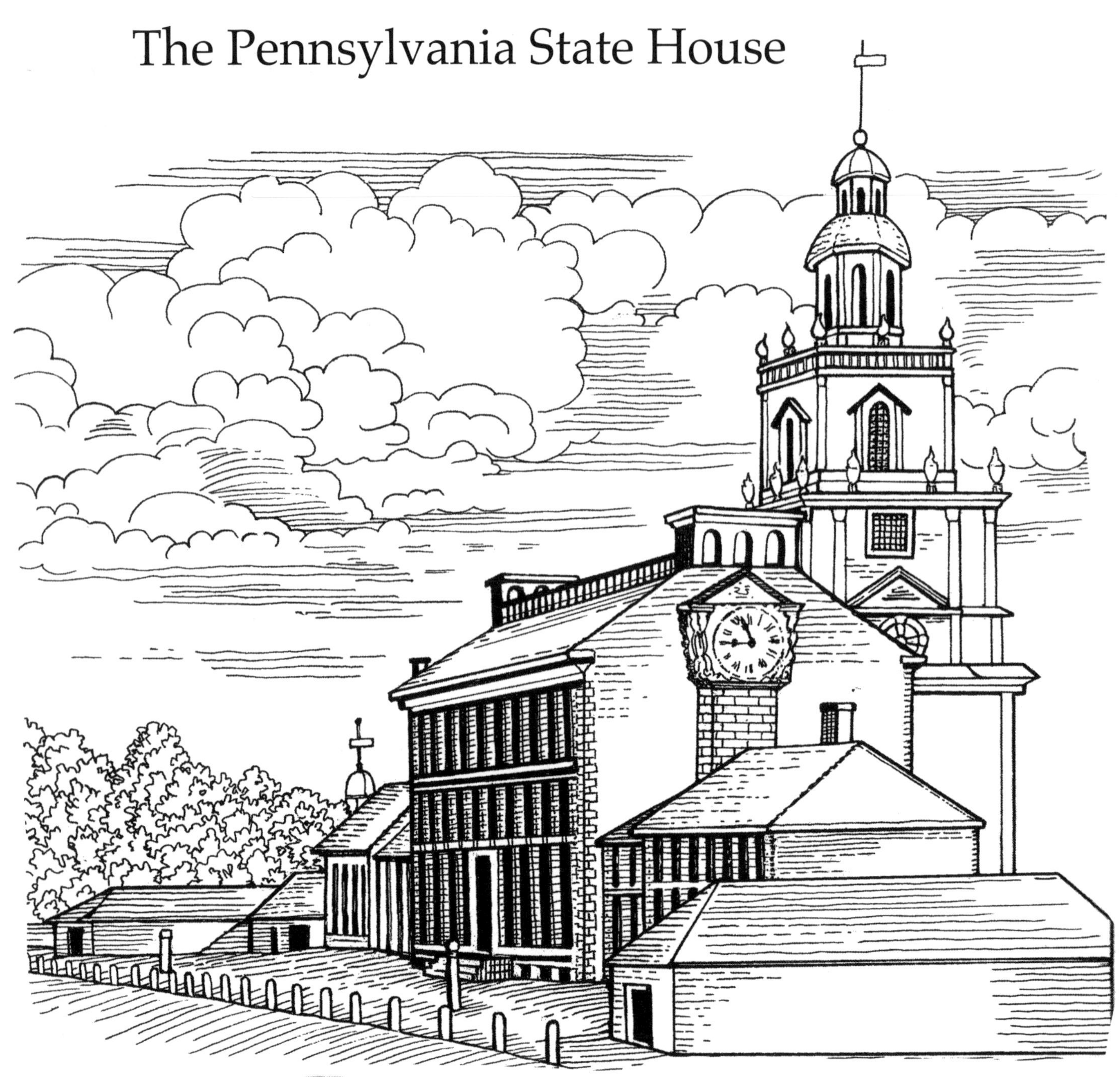

"Mr. Galloway offers the State House, & insists on Our meeting there, which he says, he has a right to offer, as Speaker of that House..."—*Silas Deane,* August 31, 1774

"...Met in (the 2nd) Congress at the State House, Chief of the members arrived, and Chose a President Mr. Randolph (again) & Secretary."—*Robert Treat Paine,* May 10, 1775

The Second Continental Congress

Convened May 10, 1775

The Delegates' entry into Philadelphia: "First appeared 2 or 300 Gentlemen on horseback preceded by the new chosen city Military Officers 2 and 2 with drawn swords followed by John Hancock and Samuel Adams in a Phaeton and pair (of horses)...Next came John Adams and Mr. Cushing in a single horse chaise...and many delegates from Congress." —*Samuel Curwen* "Bells all ringing... Shouts & Huzzas." —*Silas Deane*

carriage: bright yellow

"I was with my Friend Mr. Hancock near the Scene of Action at Lexington on the 19th of April..."—*Samuel Adams*

"This year, Mr. Hancock was added to our number."

May 10, 1775

John Hancock: "Tell me, ye bloody butchers! ye villains high and low!...Ye dark designing knaves, ye murderers, parricides! how dare you tread upon the earth...Let our misfortunes teach posterity to guard against such evils for the future...the present noble struggle for liberty will terminate gloriously for America..." March 5, 1774

John Adams: "Liberty once lost is lost forever. When the People once surrender their share in the Legislature, and their Right of defending the Limitations upon Government, and of resisting every Encroachment upon them, they can never regain it." July 7, 1775

Samuel Adams: "Genl. Washington...Let our youth look up to this Man as a pattern to form themselves by, who Unites the bravery of the Soldier, with... Modesty & Virtue." June 16, 1775

The Other Delegates from Massachusetts, Robt. T. Paine: "May the Collision of British flint and American steel produce that Spark of liberty which shall illumine the latest posterity."

Thomas Cushing to Deborah Cushing: "The (Pennsylvania) Farmer says, if it was Customary to choose Women into the Assembly, he should be heartily for choosing you Speaker of the House..." Oct 4, 1774

"The Famous Mr. Jefferson a Delegate from Virginia

in the Room of Mr. Randolph, arrived..." June 21, 1775.

Jefferson: "The abolition of domestic slavery is the great object of desire...the whole art of government consists in the art of being honest."—*Rights of British America*, 1774, published by Clementina Rind.

Washington: "I have been called upon by the unanimous Voice of the Colonies to take Command of the Continental Army."—June 20, 1775

R.H. Lee: "...happily for the cause of humanity, the Colonies are now united, and may bid defiance to Tyranny..." May 28, 1775

Patrick Henry: "The distinctions between Virginians, Pennsylvanians, New Yorkers, and New Englanders, are no more. I am not a Virginian but an American." Oct. 22, 1775

Peyton Randolph Again*

May 10 – 23, 1775

"Our President (Randolph, re-elected) left us Yesterday on Acct. of Attending as Speaker of the House of Burgesses now called in Virginia, & Mr. Hancock presides in his Room."—*Silas Deane,* May 24, 1775. Adams and Adams worked for Hancock's election after Middleton declined.

"Our country must be saved!"

*In numbering the presidents, we have followed the *Letters of Delegates to Congress, 1774–89.*

3. John Hancock

May 24, 1775 – October 29, 1777

First President of the United States of America

"Our President (Hancock) is...Noble, Disinterested & Generous to a very great Degree."—*Benjamin Harrison* to George Washington, July 21,

"...let the Footsteps of Victory open a Way for Blessings of Liberty, and the Happiness of well ordered Government...when the black and bloody Standard of Tyranny is erected..., Patriots cease to remain inactive Spectators of their Country's Fall...the Happiness, or Misery, of Millions yet unborn, is now to be determined..."—President *John Hancock,* November 30, 1775

Washington at Congress

Sept. 5 – Oct. 26, 1774
May 10 – June 23, 1775

"Mr. Lynch...told us that Colonel Washington made the most eloquent Speech at the Virginia Convention that ever was made. Says he, 'I will raise 1,000 Men, subsist them at my own Expense and march my self at their Head for the Relief of Boston.'"
—*John Adams,* August 29, 1774

"Colonel Washington appears at Congress in his Uniform and by his great Experience and Abilities in military Matters, is of much service to Us."—*John Adams,* May 29, 1775

"...the once happy and peaceful plains of America are either to be drenched with Blood, or inhabited by Slaves. Sad alternative. But can a virtuous Man hesitate in his choice?"—*George Washington,* May 31, 1775

"...the Congress have made Choice of the modest and virtuous, the amiable, generous and brave George Washingon, Esq., to be the General of the American Army, and that he is to repair as soon as possible to the Camp before Boston. This Appointment will have a great Effect in cementing and securing the Union of these Colonies..."—*John Adams,* June 17, 1775

"I am now embarked on a tempestuous ocean from whence, perhaps, no friendly harbor is to be found."
—*George Washington,* June 19, 1775

President Hancock's Marriage to Dorothy Quincy

August 28, 1775

A Symbolic Ancestor Saer de Quincy, earl of Winchester, with 24 other barons, demanded the *Magna Carta* from King John, June 15, 1215, noted Abigail Adams, also a Quincy. "The Great Charter is the act of the united nation" (*Stubbs*). It limited arbitrary power of the king.

John Adams remarked upon "The Sudden Marriage of our President, whose agreeable lady honours us with her Presence and contributes much to our good Humour, as well as to the Happiness of the President."

The Declaration of Independence

"...the Congress have judged it necessary to dissolve all Connection between Great Britain & the American Colonies, and to declare them free and independent States...The important Consequences to the American States from this Declaration of Independence, (are) considered as the Ground & Foundation of future Government."—*John Hancock,* July 6, 1776 "...there is not a more distinguished Event in the History of America, than the Declaration of her Independence - nor any that, in all Probability, will so much excite the Attention of future Ages..."—*John Hancock,* President, January 31, 1777

"The name of this Confederation shall be the 'United States of America,'"—*J. Bartlett,* July 1, 1776 "May heaven prosper the new born Republic."—*John Adams,* July 1, 1776

The Goddard Broadside of the Declaration of Independence

January 19, 1777

"The honor of printing the first copy of the Declaration with the names of the signers fell to Mary Katherine Goddard, the printer of the *Maryland Journal*." —*Letters of Delegates, 6*

"...appealing to the Supreme Judge of the world for the rectitude of our intentions do, in the name, and by the authority of the good people of these Colonies publish and declare, that these United Colonies are, and of right ought to be Free and Independent States..."

A Celebrated Correspondence

Abigail Adams, March 31: "Remember the Ladies" in new laws, and "be more favorable to them than your ancestors...If particular care and attention is not paid to the Ladies we are determined to foment a Rebellion and will not hold ourselves bound by any Laws in which we have no voice, or Representation."

"I think Women better than Men in General."
February 13, 1779

John Adams, May 26, 1776: "How then does the Right rise in the Majority to govern the Minority, against their Will? Whence arises the Right of Men to govern Women without their Consent? Whence the Right of the old to bind the Young, without theirs?... You ought to admit Women and Children: for generally Speaking, Women and Children have as good Judgement, and as Independent Minds as those men."

The Old Court House (rebuilt), York, Pennsylvania. Congress met here from September 30, 1777, until June 27, 1778.

"But we must...contend with Difficulties. By perseverence and the Blessing of God, I trust, if we continue to deserve Freedom, we shall be able to to overcome them." —*John Hancock* to George Washington, March 6, 1776.

"In short, the critical period is arrived, that will seal the Fate, not only of ourselves, but of Posterity. Whether they shall assist the generous Heirs of Freedom, or the dastardly Slaves of imperious task-Masters, it is in our Power now to determine..."—*John Hancock*, July 16, 1776

The Fite House, Baltimore, Congress's Home
December 20, 1776–February 27, 1777

"Our Worthy President Mr. Hancock has Taken Leave of Congress...He has so long held (the chair) with infinite honor..."—*Robert Morris*, October 27, 1777

To General Washington: "It is now above Two years since I have had the Honour of Presiding in Congress...but the decline of health occasion'd by so long & unremitting an Application to the Duties of my Office...have at length taught me to think of Retiring...& I have determin'd to take my Leave."—*John Hancock*, October 17, 1777

To the same: "As I propose setting out on Monday and shall go thro' Bethlehem, I must request that the Escort of Horse you so politely offered to attend me, may meet me there." October 25, 1777

A Brace of Adamses Returning to Boston from York

November 11, 1777

From a Famous Letter:

"Yesterday the greatest Question was decided, which ever was decided in America, and a greater perhaps, never was or will be decided among Men. A Resolution was passed without one dissenting Colony 'that these united Colonies, are, and of right ought to be free and independent States, and as such, they have, and of Right ought to have full Power to make War, conclude Peace, establish Commerce, and to do all the other Acts and Things, which other States may rightfully do.' You will see in a few days a Declaration setting forth the Causes, which have impell'd Us to this mighty Revolution, and the Reasons which will justify it, in the Sight of God and Man. A Plan of Confederation will be taken up in a few days.

When I look back to the year 1761, and recollect the Argument concerning Writs of Assistance (to search houses, 'the worst instrument of arbitrary power,' said Otis)... which I have hitherto considered as the Commencement of the Controversy, between Great Britain and America...I am surprised at the Suddenness, as well as Greatness of this Revolution..." —*John Adams* to Abigail Adams, July 3, 1776

"It was asked in the Reign of Charles 2nd of England, How shall we turn the Minds of the People from an Attention to their Liberties? The answer was, by making them extravagant, luxurious, effeminate...We shall never subdue them (Americans), said Bernard (governor of Massachusetts Bay from 1760) but by eradicating their manners & the Principles of their Education." —*Samuel Adams,* December 30, 1780

"I am bound home - Mr. S.A. (Samuel Adams) is with me..." November 14, 1777 —*John Adams*

"I will crawl home upon my little Pony."—*John Adams*

4. Henry Laurens

November 1, 1777 – December 9, 1778

"The Arms of the United States of America having been blessed in the present Campaign with remarkable Success (at Saratoga), Congress have resolved to recommend that one day, Thursday the 18th December next be set apart to be observed by all inhabitants throughout these States for a General thanksgiving to Almighty God."—President *Henry Laurens*, November 1, 1777

"We hourly expect confirmatory accounts of a Treaty between France and the United States of America by which our Sovereignty & Independence are acknowledged & guaranteed." May 1, 1778

from South Carolina

"Articles of Confederation (are)...now Submitted to the Wisdom of thirteen United States...Our Army under General Washington are half in Rags & half of them without Blankets..." Dec. 1, 1777 "The mismanagement of our finances I often lament, our Children will feel the effects." —*Henry Laurens*, May 6, 1778

"A recommendation is gone thither for raising some regiments of Blacks, this will I suppose lay a foundation for the emancipation...& I hope be the means of dispensing the Blessings of freedom to all the Human Race in America."—*William Whipple,* March 28, 1779. "...they resolved to raise 3000 black soldiers out of the states of Georgia and South Carolina..."—*John Collins*, March 30, 1779. "Young Coll Laurens (the President's son) is appointed the first Lt. Coll of the blacks..."—*John Armstrong,* April 3, 1779, "Thank God I had a Son, who dared to die for his Country."—*Henry Laurens*

HIS MOST CHRISTIAN MAJESTY LOUIS XVI'S MINISTER PLENIPOTENTIARY, MONSIEUR GERARD, DINES WITH CONGRESS IN PHILADELPHIA AND PRESENTS PRESIDENT LAURENS AN ACT PREPARATORY TO ACKNOWLEDGING THE INDEPENDENCE OF AMERICA, A RECENT TREATY OF ALLIANCE WITH THE 13 SWISS CANTONS, AUGUST 6, 1778.

"The arrival of the Naval force so wisely sent by His Most Christian Majesty to cooperate with the arms of these States under God promise the speedy establishment of that peace which is the object of the Alliance between the two Nations...we trust that our combined efforts will secure to independence of N . America in a peace promoting the true interests of France, America, Europe & Mankind. "—*Henry Laurens* to the Minister, drafted by W.H. Drayton, July, 1778

"Ever jealous for the dignity of Congress...I feel my own honor, and much more forcibly the honor of the Public deeply wounded by Mr. (infamous Silas) Deane's Address....I cannot...considering the manner in which Business is transacted here, remain any longer in this Chair, I now resign it." —*Henry Laurens*, December 9, 1778

"Congress were pleased to appoint me to go to the United States of Holland," to look for a loan.—*Henry Laurens,* October 24, 1779.

He left Philadelphia, was captured at sea and his papers were taken. "Henry Laurens was Committed to the Tower of London (where famous beheadings took place) on suspicion of High Treason."—*Ezekiel Cornell,* Dec. 10, 1780. "England has declared war on the States of Holland. Thus the unfortunate Capture of Mr. Laurens will probably be productive of The most fortunate event to America. —*J. Root,* March 24, 1781

5. John Jay

December 10, 1778 – September 27, 1779

Jay was sent to Congress to solve the Vermont boundary dispute. "Yesterday Mr. Laurens resigned the Chair, & this morning Congress were pleased to appoint me to succeed him..." "Let Politicians learn...to dread the least Deviation from the line of Constitutional Authority...Government once relaxed is not easily braced," he said in 1779. "Congress of the 24th (September) provid(ed) for the Settlement of all Disputes between the States of New Hampshire, Massachusetts Bay and New York relative to their Boundaries &... the People of...the New Hampshire Grants (Vermont)..." —*John Jay,* September 25, 1779.

Jay would go to Paris with John Adams, Henry Laurens (freed from the Tower), and Dr. Franklin to negotiate the "great Affair," peace treaties ending the war. "The French, if they knew as much of his negotiations as they do of mine, would very justly give the Title...Le Washington de la Negotiation...to Mr. Jay."—*John Adams,* November 30, 1782.

"The independence of America is now as fixed as fate...strive who shall do the most for his country."
September 13, 1779

from
New York

6. Samuel Huntington

September 28, 1779 – July 8, 1781

"Congress have been pleased to appoint me...to negotiate Treaties of Alliance, Amity and Commerce with Spain...Mr. Huntington of Connecticut is now president of Congress."—*John Jay*

"The United States are sincerely desirous of peace...the great object of the present defensive war on the part of the allies is to establish the independency of the united states...you are therefore to make it a preliminary article to any negotiation, That Great Britain shall agree to treat with the united states as Sovereign, free and independent."—*Samuel Huntington*, President, to John Adams, October 6, 1779

"...the Articles of Confederation & perpetual Union between the thirteen United States are formally & finally ratified by all the States. We are happy to congratulate our Constituents on this important event, desired by our Friends but dreaded by our Enemies."—*Samuel Huntington*, March 2, 1781

from
Connecticut

Celebration of Establishing The Articles of Confederation & Perpetual Union of the Thirteen United States, March 1, 1781

"The Completion of this grand Union & confederation was announced by Firing thirteen cannon on the Hill and the same number on board Captn. Paul Jones Frigate in the Harbour. At Two OClock the members of Congress, The members of the General Assembly of Pennsylvania, the president and Council of that State, the officers of the Army in Town, the officers of State and a great Number of Gentlemen waited on the President of Congress to Congratulate him on this occasion; and partook of a Collation prepared at his House for that purpose. In the evening there was a grand exhibition of fireworks at the State House, & also on board Paul Jones Frigate in the Harbour - and all the Vessels in the harbor were Decorated and illuminated on this Occasion and great joy appeared in every Countenance but those of the Disaffected."—*Thomas Rodney,* March 1, 1781

"...the only question of importance...Term (limits) of three years intended." —*T. Rodney*

From the Articles of Confederation:
Article I. The Style of this confederacy Shall be The United States of America.
Article II. Each state retains its sovereignty, Freedom and independence, and every power, Jurisdiction and right which is not by this confederation expressly delegated to the United States. In Congress assembled...

"...and at five I Dined at Mr. McKeans with the President & Vice president of this State and a number of Members of Congress & other Gentlemen and this evening we had a grand exhibition of fire Works at the State House, and another on board of Paul Jones Ship–and indeed all the Day has been Spent in rejoicing... the Confederation had enumerated Sundry things Which Should Not be done but by the Assent of nine States... much fine reasoning and Sophistry...was made use of (to have just five states approve) And indeed no Species of artful reasoning Within the reach of Lawyers was left untried on this Occasion. Here we had an opportunity to Seeing that maxim Verified 'that all men would be Tyrants if they Could git the Power' And I must Confess I was Sorry to See Such a keen Struggle to increase the power of Congress beyond What the States intended, so early as but the third day after Completing the Confederation...they would give a dreadful alarm to the Constituents Who are so jealous of their Liberty."—*Thomas Rodney*, March 1 & 5, 1781

"Baron de Montesquieu (said) that in all democratical Governments the Manners control the Laws (and that is) fully verified in the United States."—*James Varnum*, Feb. 15, 1781

Secretary Charles Thomson, Acting President

Secretary September 5, 1774 – July 25, 1789
Acting President November 4 – 10, 1779

"A people who wish to be free will ever be jealous of those to whom they entrust power."—*Charles Thomson*, March 21, 1779

"The Secretary did Business to day (in convening Congress) in the absence of the President."—*John Fell*, Nov. 4, 1779

President Huntington's term expired with all the Connecticut delegation. "...after Several Days absence Mr. Huntington resumed the Chair by general Consent and Business has proceeded as usual..."—*Nathaniel Scudder*, November 22, 1779

James Madison Reports to Congress

March 20, 1780, four days after his 29th birthday

To Thomas Jefferson: "Our army threatened with an immediate alternative of disbanding or living on free quarter, the public treasury empty, public credit exhausted... Congress complaining of the extortion of the people, the people of the improvidence of Congress, and the army of both..."—*James Madison*, March 27, 1780

"Would it not be as well to liberate and make soldiers at once of the blacks...it would Certainly be more consonant to the principles of liberty which ought never to be lost sight of in a contest for liberty."—*James Madison*, November 28, 1780

7. Thomas McKean

July 10, 1781 – November 4, 1781

Samuel Johnston of North Carolina was elected president of Congress on July 9, but he declined for bad health. Thomas McKean of Delaware was then elected. "Maryland have at length acceded to the Confederation and Perpetual Union of the United States of America...Our whole Government is now established, but it will require considerable improvements to bring it to perfection..."—*Thomas McKean,* July 26, 1781

"When the most virtuous Cause that ever a People was engaged in is conducted by consummate Prudence and Wisdom, supported by Fortitude and true Courage, and visibly favored by the Almighty, there are the surest Grounds to expect Success.—*Thomas McKean,* July 26, 1781

Later, to George Washington

"It affords me ineffable pleasure to present to Your Excellence the Thanks of the United States in Congress assembled, for the distinguished Services you have rendered to your Country, and particularly for the conquest of Lord Cornwallis...(and) that you may be ever hailed the Deliverer of your Country..."—*Thomas McKean,* President, October 31, 1781

with Thomas, Jr.

President McKean to the Comte de Rochambeau

September 4, 1781

"I have the honor to express to your Excellency the satisfaction of Congress in the compliment which has been paid to them by the Troops of his most Christian Majesty under your Command. The brilliant appearance and exact discipline of the several Corps do the highest honor to their Officers, and afford a happy presage of the most distinguished services in a cause which they have so zealously espoused."

"...the plan of the present campaign is changed from New York to the southern states... General Washington is here & a large division of the army daily passing thro...I had yesterday the pleasure to see the first division of the French. They marched through Front & Chestnut streets by the state house...the members of Congress were at the door of the state house and recd from the officers of the army as they passed a royal salute. The ceremony on their part was to let fall the point of the sword, likewise the colours, and members of Congress took off their hats. The engaging figure and behavior of the officers of all ranks, their dress, the cavalry, musick, arms, artillery, the figure & behavior of the privates, the uniform motion of the whole, afforded the most pleasing prospect of the kind I ever saw."—*S. Livermore,* Sept. 4, 1781

"As Chief Justice of this State (Pennsylvania) I shall be under a necessity of attending the Supreme Court next week...I shall therefore resign the chair of Congress." —*Thomas McKean,* October 18, 1781. He resigned October 23 but remained by request until Nov.5.

8. John Hanson

November 5, 1781–November 4, 1782

"I have the honor to inform you that this day pursuant to the Articles of Confederation, the United States in Congress assembled proceeded to the Choice of a President and have Elected for the Ensuing Year his Excellency John Hanson." —*Charles Thomson,* Secretary, November 5, 1781

"Congress can do no more than recommend...our difficulties principally arose from the want of money... Our present situation is truly Alarming..." —*J.H.,* Sept. 19, 1780

from Maryland

"The Defeat of the British fleet is a most Glorious and fortunate Event, as it will Effectually prevent Any Succors being Sent to Cornwallis, whose fate...I think is inevitable - God grant the Business may be Speedily Effected."—*John Hanson*, October 3, 1781.

"The glorious Success of the allied Arms, in the Capture of Lord Cornwallis and his whole Army on the 17th October (will be) a Day famous in the annals of American History."—*Elias Boudinot,* October 23, 1781

"Twenty four standards of Lord Cornwallis army brot to congress displayed & paraded through the city, made a most pleasing appearance..."—*Samuel Livermore,* Nov. 6, 1781.

"General Washington Arrived here last Evening...every testimony of Joy and respect will I dare Say be shewn on the Occasion...let us Strain every nerve to drive the Enemy from every part of our Country the next Campaign..."—*John Hanson*, November 27, 1781

To George Washington..."the present Aspect of our Public Affairs is particularly pleasing: And so much do we seem extricated from our perplexing difficulties, and such, I hope...we shall not relapse into our former state of imbecility and distress. The events of the present Campaign will, no doubt, fill the most brilliant pages in the history of America. May Heaven still continue to smile on our efforts!"—*John Hanson*, November 27, 1781

9. Elias Boudinot

November 4, 1782 – November 3, 1783

To George Washington: "I congratulate your Excellency and the Army, on the admission of our Independency and national Character by the Court of Great Britain." December 25, 1782

In the "late glorious Success, in a War so unequal...I have been in the midst of the principle Scenes of Action, during the whole Contest...I have carefully and attentively watched & Compared the Steps of divine Providence thro' the whole; and as the result, I can assure you, that our Success has not been the effect of either our Numbers—Power—Wisdom or Art. It has been manifestly the Effect (I was going to say the miraculous Effect) of the astonishing and unparalled interposition of a holy God in our favour...the special aid & overruling direction of Heaven."—*Elias Boudinot,* August 20, 1783

July 4, 1783, Princeton, Capitol of the United States

Dr. Witherspoon, President of the College of New Jersey and long a member of Congress, with Secretary Thomson and young collegians, about to make "Orations, one on independence the other on the advantages & disadvantages of a republican form of government...These being ended, Congress returned to their chamber (on the second floor). In the mean while preparations were making...for a grand celebration of the day." Thomson described the flag, and then, "about four there fell a deluge of rain." July 5, 1783

The Most Elegant Coach in Town
Bought by Presidents Hanson & Boudinot
Including a new sett of Harness & putting on the Public Arms
November 21, 1783
"One pair of Horses, One pipe of Madeira Wine and Two Hogsheads
of Claret for the use of said Presidents family: $1600"

"When the Enemy withdraw their forces from the Continent I shall believe they are in Earnest about peace but not until then."—*James Hanson*, August 14, 1782.

"I hope for the Best but I cant help suspecting the designs of our Rascally enemy." —.*James Hanson*, Aug. 21, 1782

10. Thomas Mifflin

November 3, 1783 – June 3, 1784

The Third Congress under the Articles of Confederation

"On the first Monday in this month the United States in Congress Assembled proceeded by ballot to the election of a President - when the honorable Thomas Mifflin was elected. Next day they adjourned Congress to meet at Annapolis in the State of Maryland on the 26th of the present month."—*Charles Thomson*, November 13, 1783

To Certain States:

"I have the honor to inform you that Mr. Thaxter, the private Secretary of Mr. Adams, arrived here from France last evening; being dispatched by our Ministers at Paris with a Copy of the definitive treaty of peace between the United States of American and Great Britain; which was signed on the 3rd of September last. I beg leave to congratulate your Excellency on this great event.."—*Thomas Mifflin*, November 23, 1783

The Maryland State House in Annapolis. Congress sat here Dec. 18, 1783– June 3, 1784.

from Pennsylvania

"To day my love the General at a public audience made a deposit of his commission and in a very pathetic manner took leave of Congress. It was a solemn and affecting spectacle; such an one as history does not present. The General's hand which held the address shook as he read it.The spectators all wept, and there was hardly a member of Congress who did not drop tears...When he commended the interests of his dearest country to almighty God, and those who had the superintendence of them to his holy keeping, his voice faultered and sunk, and the whole house felt his agitations. 'Having now finished the work assigned me I retire from the great theatre of action, and bidding an affectionate farewell to this august body under whose orders I have so long acted I here offer my commission and take my leave of all the employments of public life.' So saying he drew out from his bosom his commission and delivered it up to the president of Congress." —*James McHenry,* to Margaret Caldwell Dec. 23, 1783

11. Richard Henry Lee

November 30, 1784 – November, 1785

"It is by many here suggested as a very necessary Step for Congress to take - The calling upon the States to form a Convention for the Sole purpose of revising the Confederation so far as to enable Congress to execute with more energy, effect & vigor the powers assigned to it, than it appears by experience that they can do under the present state of things."—*R.H. Lee* to James Madison, November 26, 1784

"Good government is not the work of short time, or of sudden thought. From Moses to Montesquieu the greatest geniuses have been employed on this difficult subject..."

Later
"...the plan for us to pursue, will be to propose the necessary amendments...It having been found from universal experience, that the most express declarations and reservations are necessary to protect the just rights and liberty...from the silent, powerful and ever active conspiracy of those who govern...such precautions are necessary to restrain and regulate the exercise of the great powers given to rulers."
Oct. 16, 1787

from Virginia

Congress adjourned from Annapolis June 3, 1784 and met at Trenton October 30 at the French Arms Tavern, then went on to New York the following January. "An itinerant Congress,"—*John Mercer,* November 12, 1784. "Wandering Stars,"—*Elias Boudinot*

12. John Hancock Again

November 23, 1785 – June 5, 1786

"We found Mr. Hancock was generally thought of as President of Congress and this day he was chosen...and Mr. Ramsay to act as chairman till the President shall take the chair."—*N. Dane,* Nov. 23, 1785. Hancock wrote Nov. 30 and acknowledged the honor and that "as soon as I can Arrange my Affairs here (Boston)" he would take up the duties. "Mr. Hancock we hear is on the road & will be with us in a few days–he accepts the chair,"—*James Monroe* to James Madison, Dec. 19, 1785. "When will President Hancock come on? I long to see him & shall with great pleasure resign to him that chair which I now occupy in his absence."—*David Ramsay,* Jan. 18, 1786. "We do not get any acct. of the presidents state of health. We are therefore entirely at a loss when to expect him."—*Nathaniel Gorham,* March 6, 1786. But he was never able to return and finally wrote Congress so, on June 5, 1786. On June 6, Nathaniel Gorham was elected President.

The New Constitution (later)

"...the powers reserved by the people render them secure, and until they themselves become corrupt, they will always have upright and able rulers. I gave my assent to the Constitution in full confidence That the amendments proposed will soon become a part of the system."—*J.H.,* Feb. 6, 1788

Chairman Dr. Ramsay

"till the President (Hancock) shall take the chair."
November 23, 1785 – May 15, 1786

Col. George Mason

"There is no declaration of any kind, for preserving the liberty of the press, or the trial by jury in civil cases..."

"A plan will shortly be brought into Congress to recommend a continental convention for the purpose of enlarging the powers of Congress." May 14, 1786.

"This Constitution has been formed without the knowledge or idea of the people...it was improper to say to the people, take this or nothing."

Conventions & Amendments

Charles Pinckney of South Carolina urged "the calling of a general convention of the states, for the purpose of revising and amending the federal system," on March 13, 1786. Conventions had met in Boston, in Hartford in 1779, and in Annapolis in 1786 to discuss troubles. "A Grand Convention should be held at Philadelphia May next," it was declared, and so one met there on Monday, May 14 until November 17, 1787. "What the result of the experiment (a new constitution) may be is among the arcana of futurity. ... No hope is entertained from the existing Confederacy." —*J. Madison,* June 6, 7. "The subjects of revenue should be few, simple & well defined..." —*J. Varnum,* Aug. 4. "In the Course of four Months Severe and painful application and Anxiety, the Convention have prepared a plan of Government." —*North Carolina Delegates,* Sept. 18. But, said Col. Mason, "A new set of ideas seemed to have crept in since the articles of Confederation were established. Conventions of the people, or with power derived expressly from the people, were not then thought of...There is no Declaration of Rights," he growled, and went home "in an exceeding ill humor indeed." —*Madison,* Oct. 24. "The bill of rights will be brought forward," however, announced R.H. Lee in Congress in New York. And anon, "Virginia has set the example of opening a door for amendments." —*Madison,* Dec. 9. Later: "Col. R.H. Lee (is) relaxing in his opposition...the authority (Washington) is such as almost to overcome the improbability of the thing..."Jan 30, 1788

13. Nathaniel Gorham

Chairman May 15 to June 6, 1786, then elected President to October 22, 1787

"Congress have now before them a Motion for calling a Convention of the States to consider whether they will establish a federal Government with powers adequate to the necessities & happiness of the Union...when are we to expect Mr. Hancock?" "Unless the States make great exertion the very appearance of the Federal Government must cease."—*Nathaniel Gorham,* June 17, 1786

"Mr. Hancock has sent his resignation as President, and Tomorrow I suppose Mr. Gorham will be elected his successor."—*Rufus King,* June 4, 1786

"In such a Government as ours, it is necessary to guard against the Government itself being seduced," said Mr Gorham in the Federal Convention, August 23, 1787.

from Massachusetts

"Why does not the gentleman (R.H. Lee) propose his amendments - then the expediency of the amendments will be considered." September 27, 1787

14. Arthur St. Clair

February 2 – October, 1787

"Sir, the national Convention, to which the People look up for much good will soon rise, and it appears to be of great Consequence that when their Report comes under the consideration of Congress, it should be a full Congress and the important business which will be laid before them meet with no unnecessary Delay."—*Arthur St. Clair,* President, August 13, 1787. He was appointed governor of the North West Territory in October. William Grayson was Chairman July 4–17; President St. Clair was away westward.

"Congress (is) now looking upon the Western country...as a most valuable fund for the total extinguishment of the domestic debt..." —*William Grayson,* October 22, 1787

"Congress have authorized St. Clair now Governor of the Western territory to hold a treaty with the Indians...14,000 dollars are appropriated for this purpose."—*Wm. Grayson,* Oct. 22, 1787

"Sales of Land in the Western Territory beyond the Ohio exceed the Expectations of Congress - a Company from New England have purchased about 5 Millions of Acres in that Country."
—*L. Cadwalader,*
Oct. 23, 1787.

from
Pennsylvania

15. Cyrus Griffin

January 22, 1788 – October 31, 1788,
and in the remaining Confederation Congress November 3 to March 4, 1789

"We are now thinking of Amendments..."—*Madison* to G.W., N.Y., Feb. 1, 1788 "The proposed constitution now stands upon a firm basis; the ratification of Massachusetts will carry it triumphantly throughout...men of influence in Virginia, are relinquishing their oppositions...I hope the United States...will adopt a Constitution beautiful in theory and which will found a Government of Safety and Energy..."—*Cyrus Griffin*, February 18 and April 14, 1788. To Madison: "...indeed, my dear sir, we consider you as the main pillar of the business..." "...it seems to me the period is fully arrived to close the Confederation."—*C.G.*, April 7, 1788.

"...a fixed and efficient government should be organized with all expedition." Dec, 15, 1787

"The proposed constitution now stands upon a firm basis; The ratification of Massachusetts will carry it triumphantly throughout." Feb. 18, 1788

from Virginia

Dr. Franklin Saves the *New* Constitution

September 17, 1787

"The engrossed Constitution being read, Docr. Franklin rose with a speech in his hand...which Mr. Wilson read...'Mr. President, I confess that there are several parts of this constitution which I do not at present approve...Sir, I agree to this Constitution with all its faults, if they are such; because I think a general Government is necessary for us, and there is no form of Government but what may be a blessing to the people if well administered...I hope therefore...for the sake of posterity, we shall act heartily in recommending this Constitution...' "—*James Madison.*

"But are we to accept a form of government which we do not entirely approve of, merely in hopes that it *will* be administered well?...nothing is more liable to be abused than power. Power, without a check in *any* hands, is tyranny...there ought to be at least an express reservation of certain inherent unalienable rights, which it would be equally sacreligious for the people to *give away,* as for the government to invade." Boston, *Independent Chronicle,* Dec. 6, 1787

"Is it not my Friend... essential to every free Govt., that ye Legislative & executive Departments should be entirely distinct & independent?... Where those Powers are united, Govt.must soon degenerate into a Tyranny...I only complain & lament that that Power was not distributed in such a Manner as might preserve, instead of threaten, Destruction to ye Liberties of America." —*Rev. James Madison* to James Madison, Jr.

Kids: listen to your parents!

"I never saw him so keen for any thing in my life as he is for the new Form of Government."
—*Alexander Donald,*
October 1787

"My dear General,

At length the new govt. has received the last act necessary to its existence. This day Congress passed the requisite previous arrangements. The first Wednesday in January the ratifiying states are to appoint electors, on the first Wednesday in February the president is to be chosen, & the first Wednesday in March is the time, & this city the place for commencing proceedings...our peace & prosperity depends on the proper improvement of the present period, my anxiety is extreme that the new Govt. may have an auspicious beginning. To effect this & to perpetuate a nation formed under your auspices, it is certain that again you will be called forth..."—*Henry Lee,* New York, September 13, 1788.

"Sir...(to George Washington) I was honored with the command of the Senate to wait upon your excellency with the information of your being elected to the office of President of the United States of America..."—*Charles Thomson*, Mount Vernon, April 14, 1789.

"...I believe I cannot give a greater evidence of my sensibility for the honor they have done me, than by accepting the appointment."—*George Washington*, April 24, 1789.

General Washington and Secretary Thomson
Mount Vernon to New York in Eight Days
April 16 – 23, 1789

"Upon considering how long time some of the gentlemen of both Houses of Congress have been at New York, how anxiously desirous they must be to proceed to business, and how deeply the public mind appears to be impressed with the necessity of doing it immediately, I cannot find myself at liberty to delay my journey..."—*George Washington*

"His progress was retarded by the tender and affectionate leave which his neighbors and friends took of him; by congratulatory addresses which he was obliged to receive by the way; and by the testimonies of public esteem and joy, to which it was necessary for him to pay attention, in the several States through which he passed; but that this might occasion as little delay as possible, he commenced his journey every morning at sun-rise, continued it incessantly throughout the day, and supported the fatigues of it, eight days successively, till he reached this place (New York)." —*Charles Thomson*, April 24, 1789.

"On Thursday next the President of the United States, G. Washington is to take the Oath and enter upon the Duties of his Office."—*Hugh Williamson*, April 27, 1789.

"I have always viewed you (G.W.) as raised up by Providence to be the Saviour and father of your Country."—*Charles Thomson*, July 25, 1789.

Washington Inaugurated President

New York City, April 30, 1789

"I was summoned by my Country, whose voice I can never hear but with veneration and love...it would be peculiarly improper to omit in this first official Act, my fervent supplications to that Almighty Being who rules over the Universe, who presides in the Councils of Nations, and whose providential aids can supply every human defect, that his benediction may consecrate to the liberties and happiness of the People of the United States, Government instituted by themselves...No People can be bound to acknowledge and adore the invisible hand, which conducts the Affairs of men, more than the People of the United States. Every step, by which they have advanced to the character of an independent nation, seems to have been distinguished by some token of providential agency...the foundations of our National policy will be laid in the pure and immutable principles of private morality, and the pre-eminence of a free Government, be exemplified by all the attributes which can win the affections of its Citizens, and command the respect of the world...I dwell on this prospect since...the propitious smiles of Heaven, can never be expected on a nation that disregards the eternal rules of order and right, which heaven itself has ordained. And since the preservation of the sacred fire of liberty, and the destiny of the Republican model of Government, are justly considered as deeply, perhaps as finally staked, on the experiment entrusted to the hands of the American people."